GOING TO THE MOON

JAMES MUIRDEN
ILLUSTRATED BY NIGEL CODE

Kingfisher Books

Advisers: Mary Jane Drummond, Tutor in
Primary Education, Cambridge Institute of
Education, Cambridge
Iris Walkinshaw, Headteacher, Rushmore Infants
School, Hackney, London.
Patricia Brown, Children's Librarian, North
Kensington Library, London
Photograph: Dr Fred Espenak/SPL 31

First published in 1987 by Kingfisher Books
Limited, Elsley Court, 20–22 Great Titchfield
Street, London W1P 7AD
A Grisewood & Dempsey Company.

BRITISH CATALOGUING IN PUBLICATION DATA
Muirden, James
Going to the moon.—(Stepping stones 4, 5, 6)
1. Moon—Juvenile literature
I. Title   II. Code, Nigel III. Series
523.3   QB582
ISBN: 0 86272 252 7

Edited by Vanessa Clarke
Designed by Nicholas Cannan
Cover designed by Pinpoint Design Company
Phototypeset by Southern Positives and Negatives (SPAN),
Lingfield, Surrey
Printed in Spain.

Contents

4

Here is the full moon, rising into the sky.
Some people say they can see a Man in the
Moon with two eyes and an open mouth.
But there is not really a Man in the Moon.
The dark patches which look like eyes and
a mouth are empty, dusty plains.

The moon is not always full. Sometimes it looks like a thread of silver. Sometimes it looks like a banana or a wedge of cheese. But the moon is not really changing shape. It is always the same shape.

New moon (invisible)   Young crescent   Half moon

The moon is round like a ball. It shines because the sun lights it up. We see only the part of the moon that the sun shines on, the bright part. So the moon seems to grow from a crescent to a full moon, then to become thin again.

Full moon   Half moon   Old crescent

Out in space, the earth and moon and sun look like this. The moon is travelling around the earth all the time, day and night. Once around the earth takes a month. The earth is travelling around the sun all the time and once around the sun takes a year.

If there was a road to the moon, it would take 15 years to walk there. But there is no road. There is only empty space between the earth and the moon, and so only spacecraft can go there. This book is about the first journey from the earth to the moon.

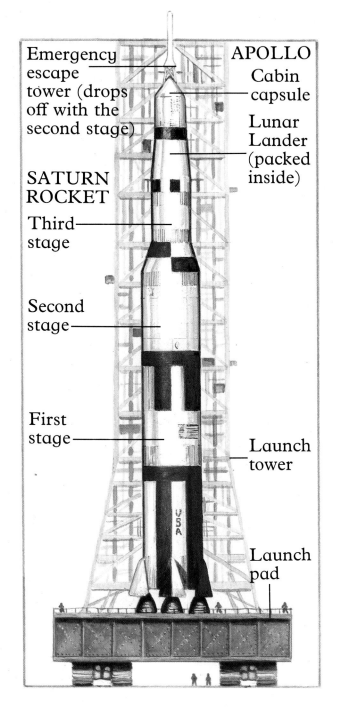

Emergency escape tower (drops off with the second stage)

APOLLO
Cabin capsule

Lunar Lander (packed inside)

SATURN ROCKET

Third stage

Second stage

First stage

Launch tower

Launch pad

USA

On July 16, 1969, the first people to go to the moon walked into a lift at the Kennedy Space Center in Florida, the United States of America.

The lift carried them up the launch tower to the spacecraft Apollo. Apollo was attached to the top of a huge rocket called Saturn. The rocket had three sets of engines and three fuel tanks, called stages.

The three astronauts squeezed into the cabin of the spacecraft and strapped themselves in, ready for the launch.

"10, 9, 8, 7, 6, 5, 4, 3, 2, 1, zero, we have lift-off!" shouted the controller. With a terrific roar the rocket blasted off from the launch pad.

Lift-off + 3 minutes
First stage away!

Lift-off + 6 minutes
First stage splashes down

Lift-off + 9 minutes
Second stage away!

The rocket hurled the spacecraft into space.
The first two rocket stages burnt up their
fuel and fell away into the Atlantic Ocean.
Now the astronauts were in orbit around
the earth.

The spacecraft orbited the earth once. Then the astronauts fired the rocket in the third stage to send the spacecraft towards the moon.

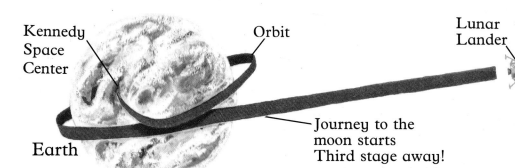

We went to the moon backwards, pulling the Lunar Lander behind us.

Kennedy Space Center

Orbit

Lunar Lander

Apollo

Earth

Journey to the moon starts Third stage away!

It was a strange journey. There was no day and no night because the sun shone on the spacecraft all the time. The astronauts had to work, eat and sleep at the times shown on their timetable.

The first job was to unpack the Lunar Lander. The astronauts joined it to the nose of the spacecraft so that it would be ready when they arrived at the moon. They left the third stage of the rocket behind in space.

Moon

Time for a sleep. We'll get an alarm call from earth to wake us up.

Inside the cabin, anything which was loose floated about because in space nothing has any weight. The astronauts had to tie themselves into the seats with a belt, or wedge themselves into corners.

The astronauts could not eat ordinary food because the crumbs might float away and jam the controls. Instead they ate food which had been pressed into cubes. They sucked drinks from plastic squeeze bottles.

The cabin of Apollo was filled with air. The astronauts had to take air with them because there is no air in space. There is no air on the moon either, and it is much hotter on the moon than anywhere on the earth.

Earth

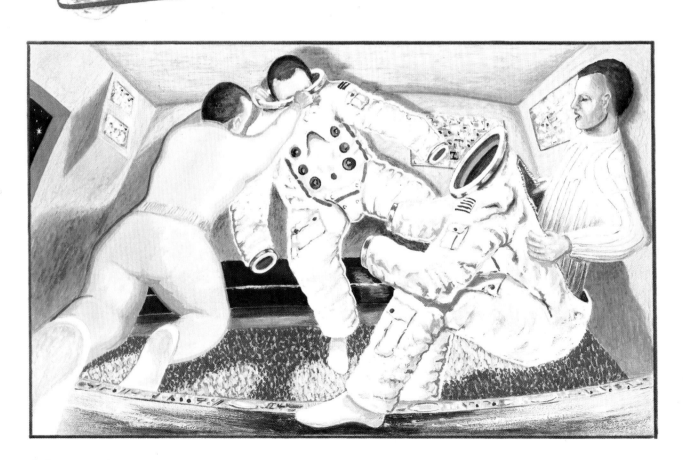

Moon

Apollo

Orbit

Time to get dressed for landing. It will take us at least an hour.

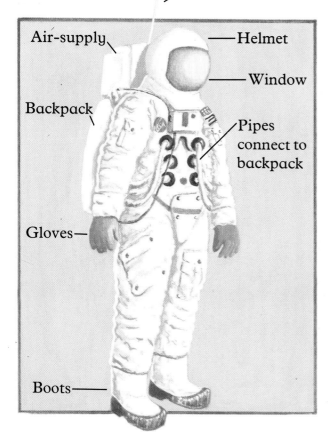

Radio aerial

Air-supply

Helmet

Window

Backpack

Pipes connect to backpack

Gloves

Boots

The astronauts had to wear protective clothing for the moon landing. To keep cool they wore undersuits which had tiny tubes sewn all over them. Cold water was pumped through the tubes.

Next they put on thick space suits. The astronauts helped each other to wriggle into them, and zipped them up. Then they fixed their gloves and helmets in place.

Only two of the astronauts would land on the moon. The third astronaut stayed behind to look after the spacecraft.

15

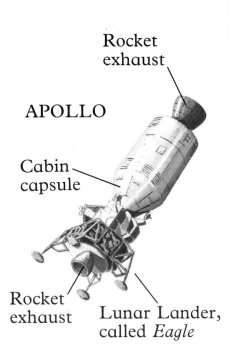

APOLLO

Rocket exhaust

Cabin capsule

Rocket exhaust

Lunar Lander, called *Eagle*

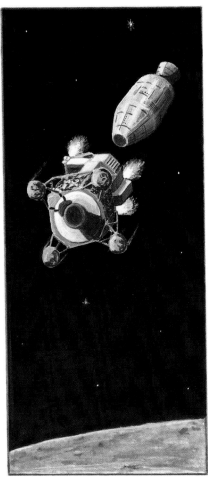

When they reached the moon, the astronauts put Apollo into orbit around the moon. Then two astronauts crawled into the Lunar Lander which they called *Eagle*. They fired its rocket engine and moved away from the spacecraft towards the moon.

16

When they were close to the surface, the astronauts fired the rocket engine again to keep flying just above the rocks. They had to find a smooth landing place. Just before the engine ran out of fuel, they touched down in a cloud of dust. They radioed: "The *Eagle* has landed!"

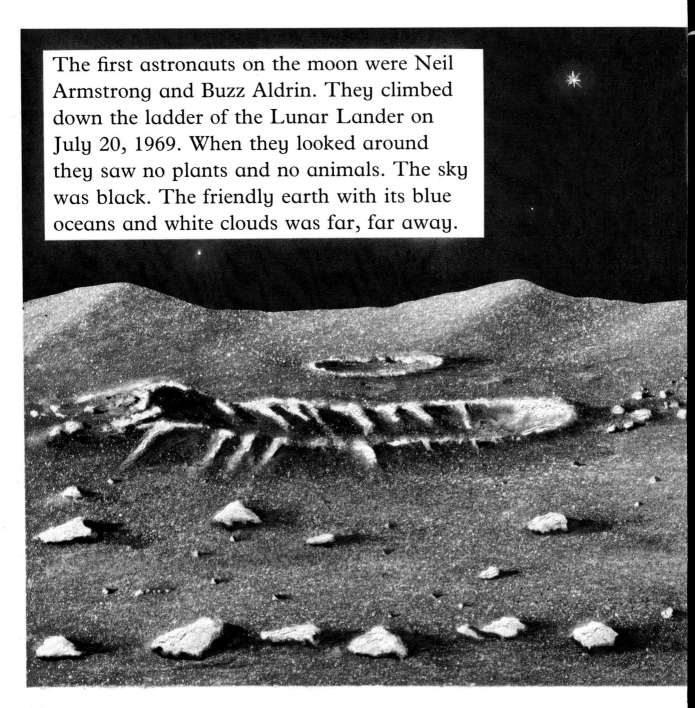

The first astronauts on the moon were Neil Armstrong and Buzz Aldrin. They climbed down the ladder of the Lunar Lander on July 20, 1969. When they looked around they saw no plants and no animals. The sky was black. The friendly earth with its blue oceans and white clouds was far, far away.

When they started to move around, the astronauts walked with a kangaroo hop. They felt light and bouncy because on the moon everything and everybody weighs much less than on the earth.

The astronauts collected rocks and dust. They had to pick them up in scoops with long handles because they could not bend over in the stiff suits.

Wherever they went, the astronauts made footprints in the moon dust. This fine dust has been falling from space for millions of years. On the earth, winds blow the dust about and rain washes it away. But there is no wind or rain on the moon because there is no air. So the astronauts' footprints are still there now, in exactly the same places.

From the earth the moon looks silvery or yellow or sometimes blue. But the astronauts found that everything around them was dark grey. Some of the rocks and dust which the astronauts brought back are in museums now, and they look grey too.

23

The first astronauts did not walk far from the Lunar Lander. But other astronauts on later journeys took a Lunar Buggy with them. The Buggy used electric batteries because petrol engines will not work without air.

The last astronauts on the moon drove 35 kilometres in the Buggy to look at some of the moon's craters. The moon is covered with craters. Some are as small as a garden but others are bigger than London. Some craters have mountains in the middle.

These craters were made millions of years ago by rocks which came crashing into the moon from space. These rocks are called meteoroids. Sometimes tiny meteoroids shoot through the air around the earth with a flash. These are called shooting stars.

The first astronauts spent only three hours on
the moon. Then they packed the moon rocks
and moon dust into *Eagle* and fired the rocket
engine. Soon Mike Collins in the cabin of
Apollo saw them flying towards the spacecraft.

When the Lunar Lander and the spacecraft had docked together, the astronauts crawled back into the cabin. They did not need *Eagle* any more so they disconnected it. They left it going around the moon on its own.

Now the astronauts fired Apollo's rocket engine and started for home. As they came near the earth they had one last job to do. They separated the cabin from the rest of the spacecraft. Only the cabin capsule with the astronauts inside came back to the earth.

As the capsule rushed through the air around the earth, it started to glow with heat. It looked like a shooting star with a fiery tail. Soon, the parachutes opened with a jerk and slowed the capsule down. Then splashdown!
The dangerous journey was over.

Between 1969 and 1972, six crews of Apollo astronauts went to the moon. They brought back enough moon rocks and moon dust to fill ten rucksacks. They left boxes of equipment which kept sending radio messages to the earth long after the astronauts had come home. But their batteries are dead now.

On this photograph of the moon the light patches are craters and mountains, and the dark patches are dusty plains. The numbers show where all the Apollo spacecraft landed.

There have been no visitors to the moon since 1972. But there are still twelve sets of footprints in the grey dust. Perhaps other footprints will join them one day, when astronauts visit the moon again.

APOLLO LANDING SITES

1 **Apollo 11**	July 20, 1969	4 **Apollo 15** July 31, 1971
2 **Apollo 12**	November 19, 1969	5 **Apollo 16** April 20, 1972
3 **Apollo 14**	February 5, 1971	6 **Apollo 17** December 11, 1972

Apollo 1–1 were test flights. Only **Apollo 8–10** carried astronauts but they did not land on the moon. There was an explosion on **Apollo 13**. The astronauts returned safely to earth without landing on the moon.

Index

Where to see moonrocks

The only moonrock in this country is at the Geological Museum, Exhibition Road, London SW7.

You can see an Apollo Cabin Capsule, a Lunar Lander, space suits and models of rockets at the Science Museum, Cromwell Road, London SW7.

Some other large museums have displays on spacecraft, rockets and space suits but not the ones used on the Apollo landings.